# Ink Zero

# *Ink Zero*
## Contemporary Haiku

Richard Gilbert

Don Baird

Ink Zero Press
Burbank, California
2015

Ink Zero Press
1600 W Magnolia Blvd
Burbank, California 91506

# *Ink Zero*

Contemporary Haiku

Copyright 2015

All rights reserved. No part of this book may be reproduced in any form or by any means, except by a reviewer or scholar who may quote brief passages in a review or article.

Authors: Richard Gilbert
Don Baird
Production Assistant/Editor: Diana Ming Jeong
Cover Design: Don Baird
Photography: Maria Baird

Printed in the United States of America
2015

Published by Ink Zero Press
Burbank, California USA

ISBN #: 978-0-578-16139-6

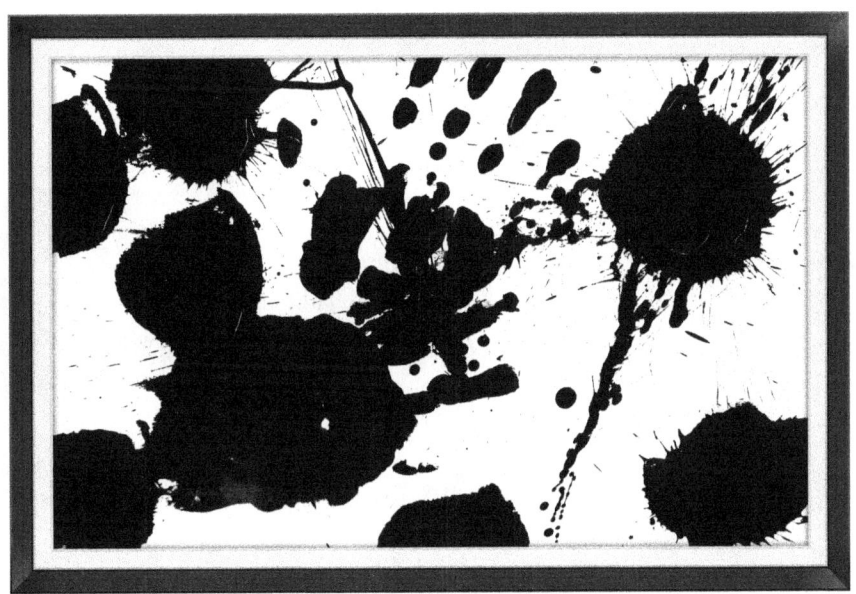

Ink Art by Richard Gilbert

# PREFACE

On a day in the ancient past (about a year ago), I arrived in Burbank, California, to visit Grandmaster Don Baird at his Dojo. The prevailing winds of cosmic forces were in good order, as we spontaneously designed the performance event "For a Day," combining Tai Ch'i demonstration with haiku by several of the 135 poets found in *The Disjunctive Dragonfly* (2013) and Don's 2014 collection, *Haiku: The Interior and Exterior of Being*. Our concept was to present haiku as collaborative in terms of both performance and authorship. Live music was provided by Rick (shakuhachi) and Kath Abela Wilson, with Mariko Kitakubo (both, on gongs and percussion). Here, a "day" of poetry was presented in four sections of dawn/morning, afternoon, twilight, and night/prophecy. The piece was once again performed, with new haiku selections, at the USC Museum in Pasadena, when I returned to the area some six months later, in September 2014.

I must return to Japan soon once again for an unknown amount of time—I am able to visit the States while on literary research grants, and my present grant ends this month—this fact raises the issue of poignancy—as our friendship and collaboration has developed, as our creative energies have entwined and blossomed, so has time moved in great leaps of months and years between opportunities for embodied creation, versus the virtuality of email and distance across oceans.

Yet, today I write having performed with Don our new collaborative piece, "Ink Zero" just last night—from which arose the book you now hold in your hands. A divine wind of synergy once again seems to blow through our lives: when I arrived a week ago Don was putting together a book of new poems, and I'd organized my own selected haiku, some 90 poems. Together we printed and cut our works into separate poems, laying them out on the dining room table. It became clear as we examined our combined works that inventive "conversations" could happen between them. You can witness the result of this play in the photos presented between the final section.

The origin of the term "ink zero" was the result of a brainstorming session we had towards the end of my September 2014 visit—at the time, we had thought it might possibly make a good journal title (still might)—so the term was kicking around, and we both came up with "ink zero" haiku, plus a further thought: to create calligraphic (*shodo*) brush-stroke paintings in the Japanese style, using sumi-e ink on drawing paper. These works likewise appear here.

It's our hope that the joy and creative friendship we've experienced in weaving our hearts and minds together with poetry and visual art communicate both the spontaneity and the successive series of excessively late nights which have hatched this project. Without the energy and flow—the mysterious threading and wending of collaborative friendship—we would have each produced separate works. Instead, we find our combined effort approaches an alpha and omega of mutual lives: living whole, and for the day. It's this poignant and ephemeral spirit we wish to share, and offer our experiment here as one possible approach to haiku publication.

Richard Gilbert
March 17, 2015

## Note to Reader

The initials of the poet are on the lower corner of the poet's haiku page.

rg for Richard Gilbert
db for Don Baird

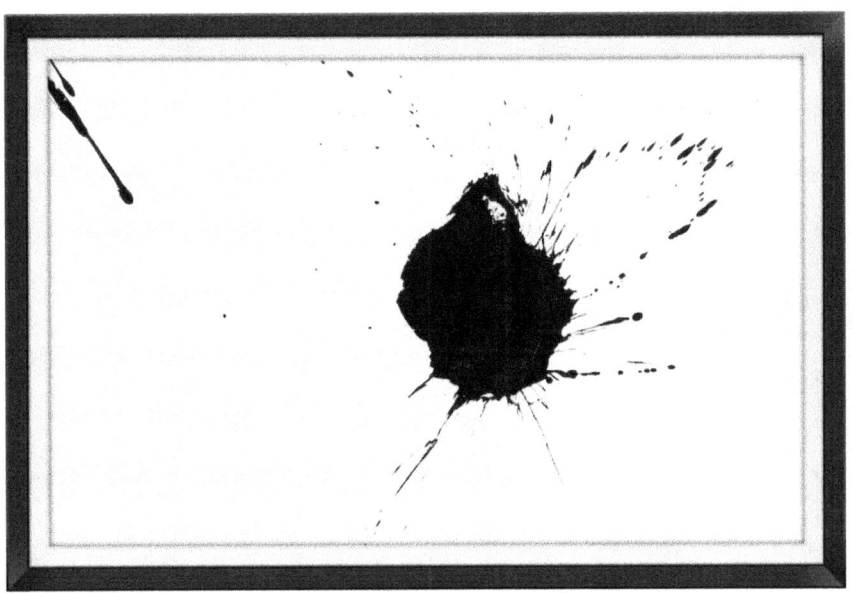

Ink Art by Don Baird

# Between Blossoms

between blossoms
the salient ebb
of creation




unaware star after star




db

stars
in the natural night
one song threads another


ink zero    murmurs

    'in –

        fin –

           i –

ty'

    bell-cricket

rg

ink zero the white blanks of a forest

db

breath skybreath stars tend towards home

rg

in the abyss a moon falling

db

new places promised shared underleaf

rg

falling through angles shadow play

db

eventually
depth penetrating
desire  s

long reach shadow nears itself

db

deep in woods
all the dancing in
space

rg

between worlds
an ant navigates
the others

db

awaiting the warm that everyone

rg

impermanence the seedling anyway

db

flower of space one can touch about moss

rg

between lights lights the way

db

iterative reconstruction the nation of stars

rg

snowbound shadows themselves




















shrinking emptiness pond-clouds nightfall









db

Ink Art by Richard Gilbert

# Butterflies and Bones

morning fog
the morning after
morning

db

on the shores of great silence father's eyes

rg

rising tide . . .
the waterfall gives birth
to a hummingbird

db

something of a scar
of ocean left
rolling cigarettes

high diving;
a hummingbird
turns away

waning gibbous
the increasing density
of fall

rg

the wind between never leaves

db

returning bones
a stone unwinds
in the breeze

rg

horizontal seashore along the mast

db

along the slice
        of water and sky
    never at night

rg

settling . . .
a butterfly in the midst
of itself

db

Please feel free to stay here
there's a system you
always said that.

rg

turning leaves . . .
a light breeze
in the sails

the sudden sliver of noon

rg

~ dangling . . .
a dandelion
doesn't know ~

db

blood orange:
the curving radius
of sunset

rg

high road between clouds dusk musk

db

solitude
round the frequency
of stars

rg

moon   cricket   autumn's wide-angle-song




jack rabbit —
the startled trail
of moonlight


db

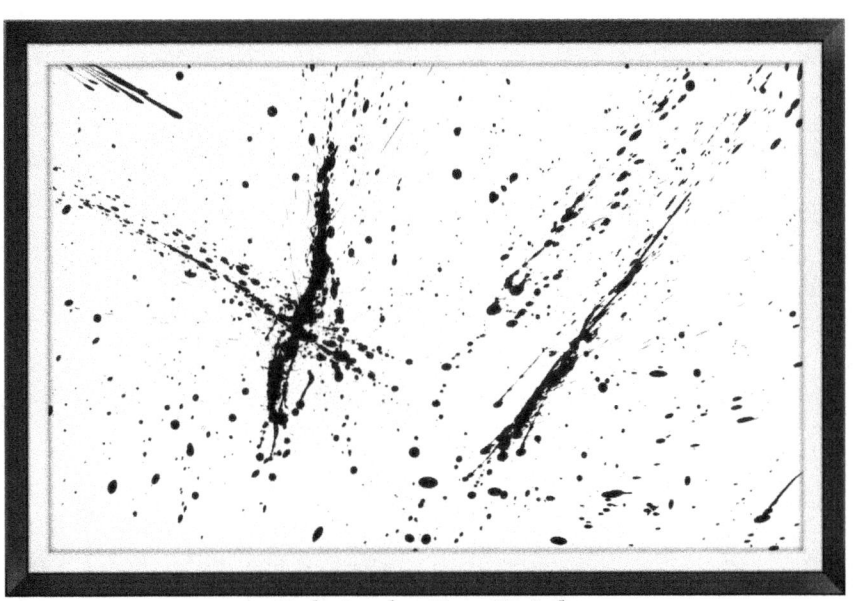
Ink Art by Don Baird

# Born of a Flower

as an and you and you and you alone in the sea

rg

this    that    then crickets

db

only so long for so long only for more

rg

inertia between thoughts another

db

depth penetrates desire s un

rg

exigent road into itself self

db

that the thine that becomes the subject
of one stroke no as if

undertow thoughts of thoughts today too

db

born of a flower of space that one touch can read
about now

rg

cumulus
accumulating
my eyes

db

a drowning man
pulled into violet worlds
grasping hydrangea

spring run-off
where does the water go
across my mind?

db

edge broke mill tooth saw diamond shattered breath

hanging mirror the shape of my thoughts

db

roses in the rose messaged and left

looking through me my reflection too

db

part icles of cha ng e le an h ar d on  on  e  b  lu e da  y  o    n

rg

see-saw
a cloud appears
not to know

db

the blood
the horse i was, left
to the woods

rg

chilled bones then the moon and not

db

after the rent
dinner raw ocean
waves

winter frost
a cloud hesitates
. . . too

db

unchangeability —
i leave the earth
that way

rg

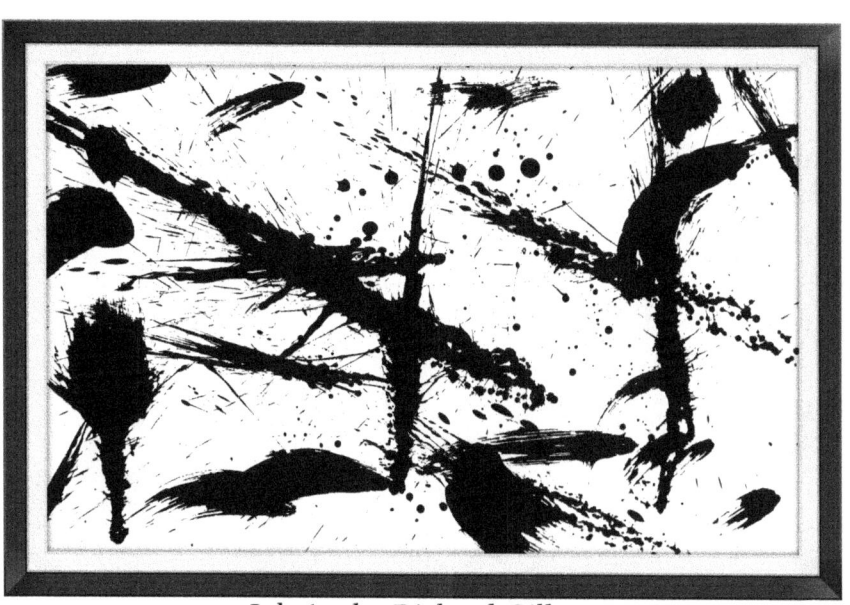

Ink Art by Richard Gilbert

# Body Born

the girl brief. image
and truth. why and
why not. about it.

moon cradled you recall the voice of another
i might be the distance

her tears the cost of a stamp

db

there in the trees to begin with just before
and just after love

rg

and then then the rain silent

db

lovecode the ultrasound of your photons

rg

dried in rain her ego

db

then     nude
normal silence
between  fears




sheeting rain
voices softer
as i well

rg

snowflakes
lingering sounds
of glances

db

what became deeper of you i let in

rg

boding well the last meteor I couldn't see

db

licking the cleft sweet aspirin after rain

rg

shallow mallow
the sunset hues of
eternity

db

about it on the beach by the trees
two moments between that is

rain repeating words repeating

db

as a body born of words
as a body bones of words:
preoccupations she writes




barely caught her breath on medium




rg

inside a tear what remains of winter

db

living
pressure of the sun
in her belly




                                        our yesterday behind the blinds



rg

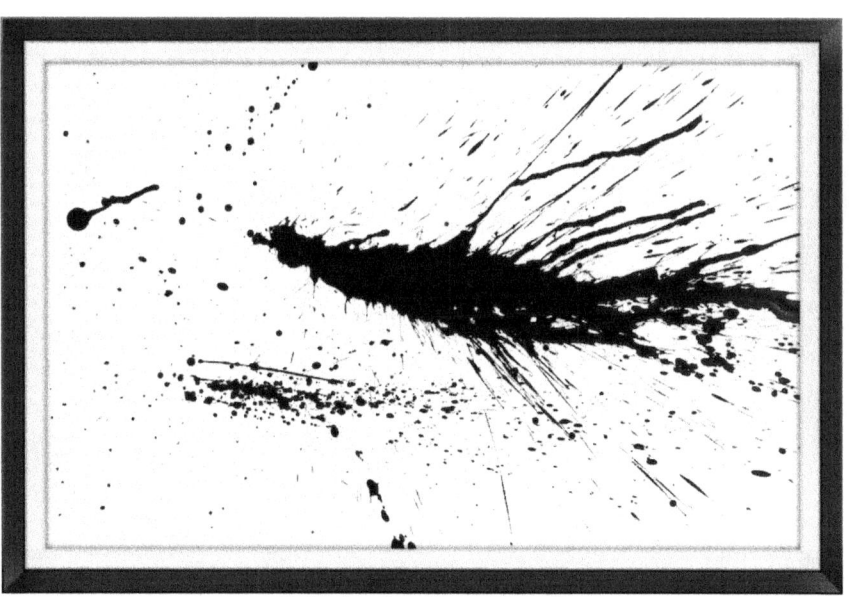

Ink Art by Don Baird

# Before and After

twin towers:
at their feet, the origami
of autumn

db

be mine —
alive for one
more war



broken whole:
worth a world
destoned

rg

desert storm banana around the feeling

db

semite war
unharmed olives — the desert
tastes your skin

rg

themselves leaves winter orange

db

it must be how
violence in the world
crocus

rg

lost and found the war before and after

db

war particles of the garbage patch










mass


solitude
what's left
of the party


denial

rg

memorial day;
the mixed messages
of a gunshot

if only lie —
hours
of a parking lot




flown,
her grainy image resolves
from surveillance

rg

Mt. Fuji;
ashes of a soldier well up
in the storm

db

running forever
spring after
tragedy




three oceans
exported into orbit
in a small cocoon

rg

fallen shopping cart autumn's home

db

trading the past
life regression for a
past life: rape

U S A prime time junkyard banner

db

unable to find
the cry of the nextdoor boy
spring rain

rg

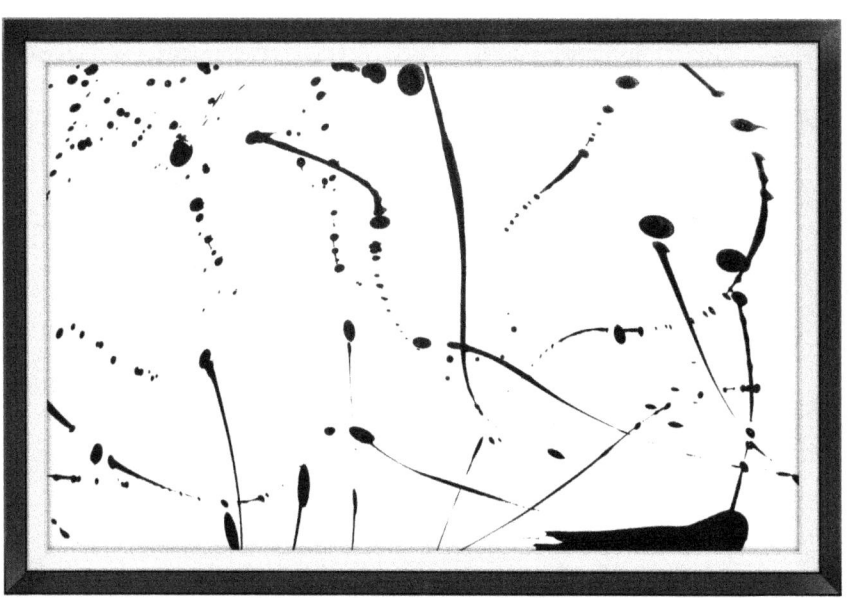
Ink Art by Richard Gilbert

# Bamboo Slam

dedicated to the moon
I rise
without a decent alibi

                r



        Madonna even so nearby ants

                        d

near her lips the glossy side

d

leaning against
the next semester her
blog in mine

r

for so long only for so long for

                                                      r



transient breath the last ah-haaa

                                                            d

weirdly insistent the matter of rain

d

everything you think i think is true

r

time fuck shit piss blue mine love mend leaf kiss must call

                                                                                  r


hanging on    hanging    hang

                            d

without you moon the loneliness

moon resins —
sex and god and teeth
and fingernails

with you and i the world
             i feel there is more f
             it

                              r


at the end
of a bamboo shoot
blue whale

              d

without thought a bird anyway

d

no eye no ear no nose no tongue no virgin no mind

r

unbound teeth not everything still her taste

r

under threat he pisses a poem

d

long long coma    I R S

                      d

hung over  -  ignoble  
Jerusalem  -  cactus  
pissing    -  the cats

            r

collateral damage scattered alpha d bits

r







names the smoke rings of pieces

d

blue daisy no name along

d

forgotten flowers
lost in
dogs

r

unabsolved ululation
uncalculated underscore
unwept unchurch ultrapure

r

big fish
in a little pond
sinking clouds

d

worm moon moving earth

                              d

apple-snap
autumn brisk
of a crush

              r

after the rush
the hollow sound
of the holy

r

without the moon my shadow and I

d

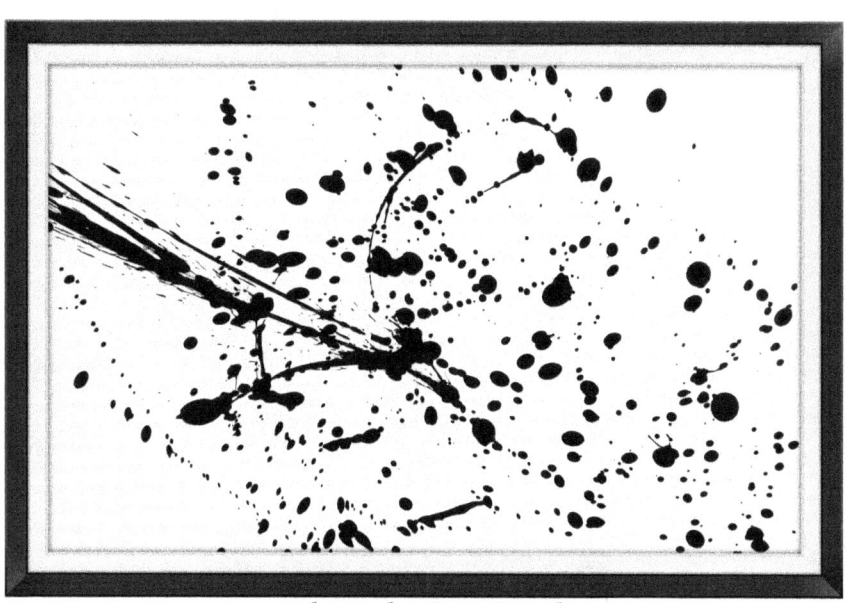

Ink Art by Don Baird

# About the Authors

## *Richard Gilbert*

Education. While at Naropa University (Boulder, Colorado), studied and hung out with beat poets Allen Ginsberg, Gregory Corso, Peter Orlovsky, Gary Snyder, and others; became a Tibetan Buddhist meditator. Performed in and produced conceptual art multidisciplinary presentations as poet, videographer, and electric guitarist. Undergraduate thesis on Japanese classical haiku, BA in Poetics and Expressive Arts, 1982. Completed Tibetan Buddhist seminary training in 1984, and returned to Naropa for an MA in Contemplative Psychology, graduated 1986. Worked as a clinical adult outpatient psychotherapist at Boulder Community Mental Health Center. In 1990, completed a Ph.D. at The Union Institute & University, in Poetics and Depth Psychology, studying Archetypal Psychology with James Hillman. Moved to Kumamoto, Japan, in 1997, teaching at university and publishing academic articles on Japanese and English-language haiku, while designing EFL educational software. Received tenure as an Associate Professor of British and American Literature, Faculty of Letters, Kumamoto University in 2002; promoted to Professor, 2015.

Activities. Co-judge of the Kusamakura International Haiku Competition, Kumamoto, Japan (2003-present). Founder and Director of the Kon Nichi Haiku Translation Group, Kumamoto University (2002-present). Founding Associate Member of The Haiku Foundation (*thehaikufoundation.org*). In March 2008, publication of *Poems of Consciousness: Contemporary Japanese & English-language Haiku in Cross-cultural Perspective* (Red Moon Press, 2008, 306 pp.) was awarded the HSA 2009 Mildred Kanterman Award for Haiku Criticism and Theory. In mixed media publication, the *gendaihaiku.com* website presents subtitled video interviews with notable *gendaihaiku* (modern Japanese haiku) poets, biographical information and haiku translations. In 2011, publication of *Ikimonofūei: Poetic Composition on Living Things* (a talk by Kaneko Tohta, with commentary and essays. Gilbert, et al, Red Moon Press, 92 pp.), and *The Future of Haiku*, an Interview with Kaneko Tohta (with commentary and essays. Gilbert, et al, Red Moon Press, 138 pp.). In 2012, publication of *Selected Haiku of Kaneko Tohta, Part 1, 1937-1960* (with commentary, essays and chronology. Gilbert, et al, Red Moon Press, 256 pp.), and *Selected Haiku of Kaneko Tohta. Part 2, 1961-2012* (with commentary, chronology and encyclopedic glossary. Gilbert, et al, Red Moon Press, 250 pp.). The two 2012 *Selected Haiku of Kaneko Tohta* volumes were awarded The Haiku Foundation 2012 Touchstone Distinguished Book Award. In August 2013, publication of *The Disjunctive Dragonfly: A New Theory of English-language Haiku* (R. Gilbert, Red Moon Press, 132 pp.): A revised and expanded update of the decade-old essay, which first appeared (in North America) in *Modern Haiku Journal 35:2* (2004). The book contains 275 haiku by 185 authors, and several new sections, including a comparative discussion of strong and weak styles of disjunction in excellent haiku, and a presentation of seven newly coined "strong reader-resistance" disjunctive categories. (Full bio. here <*http://bit.ly/1bPcrGV*>).

SHAO NPO – Mission Japan. In 2014 the NPO, Sailing for Haiku Across Oceans, was founded, and the literary-research vessel, Stella Aurore (a 35' Jeanneau Sun-Rise) was acquired for "Mission Japan," a sailing pilgrimage around Japan to meet with haiku groups countrywide, and create international poetic interchange through translation and publication. The Mission will begin September 2015 and continue throughout 2016. For more information, please visit <*http://sailing-across-oceans.org*>.

## *Don Baird*

Background.

Shortly after his birth, Don moved with his family to live on his grandfather's ranch in Wyoming. He lived in an old converted chicken coop building for some time. Eventually, he and his family moved to San Diego, California and remained there until he was 19. At 15, Don entered the world of martial arts of which remains his primary career today. He has been featured in most of the prominent industry magazines including *Inside Kung Fu, Black Belt, Inside Karate, and Fighting Stars*. In 2009 he, as a Grandmaster, was inducted into the Masters Hall of Fame. He was also featured in two police defensive tactics videos.

Education.

Graduate of UCLA in Music Performance and Education. Studied clarinet under the guidance of Dan Magnusson and Mitchell Lurie. English minor. 10th Degree Black Belt in martial arts.

Activities.

Published in numerous anthologies and online journals including *Ambrosia: Journal of Fine Haiku, Simply Haiku Journal, World Haiku Review, Notes from the Gene, Haijinx, Modern Haiku, the Heron's Nest, Frogpond, A Hundred Gourds*, and others. Placed 3rd two years in a row in the Kusamakura International Haiku Contest, (2004, 2005). Awarded 1st place in the 2009 NHK Radio International Haiku Contest: winning haiku was read by Sokan Tadashi Kondo as part of the radio program. In 2013, won the Haiku Now! International Haiku Contest. Received The Haiku Foundation Touchstone Award, 2013. Published six books of which *Haiku - the Interior and Exterior of Being* is most recent.

Current Projects.

Under the Basho Haiku Journal; *underthebasho.com*
Living Haiku Anthology; *livinghaikuanthology.com*

# Publication Credits

## Richard Gilbert

Most of my haiku presented here have been published in books and journals, including: *Haiku in English* (Kacian et al, Norton 2013); *Haiku 21* (Gurga & Metz, Modern Haiku Press, 2011); *Haiku 2014* (Gurga & Metz, Modern Haiku Press, 2013); *Bones Haiku Journal* <bonesjournal.com>; *Frogpond Journal* <hsa-haiku.org/frogpond>; *Is/Let Haiku Journal* <isletpoetry.wordpress.com>; *Moongarlic Haiku Journal* <moongarlic.org>; *Noon: Journal of the Short Poem* <noonpoetry.com>; *Rattle: Poetry for the 21st Century* <rattle.com>; and *Roadrunner Haiku Journal* <bit.ly/1AvJ8kw>.

## Don Baird

My haiku are written for *Ink Zero*. They are not published elsewhere.

## Enjoy the Following Adendum
(our creative process at work)


These photos were taken of Richard and Don while they were painting Ink Art for this book. In a few instances, there was more ink on the artists than the paintings!

Other photos are of the creative process between Richard and Don during their meeting to arrange haiku for their presentation of the *Champagne Pour Deux* and *In A Day* live performance readings. Haiku were everywhere. Soon, it was done — both shows ready and voices being cleared.

Deep Concentration

One Whip of the Brush

The Official Drying Station

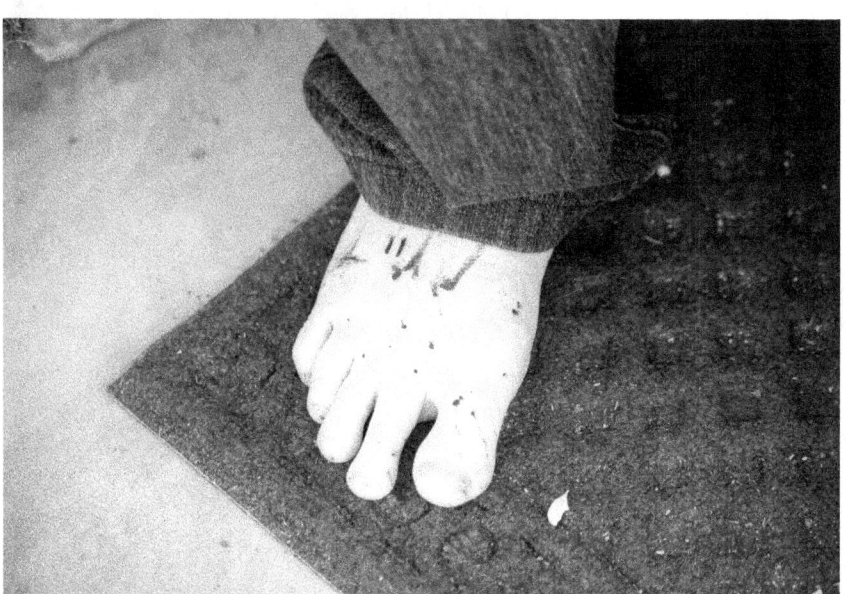
Richard's Ink Foot

Palmed by Richard

Brushes Taking a Break

Awaiting the Perfect Moment

Crouching Tiger

Don Throwing Ink

A Walk to the Drying Room

Preparing the Presentation -- *Champagne Haiku Pour Deux*

Last Minute Thoughts

# Between Blossoms
## (Spaces)

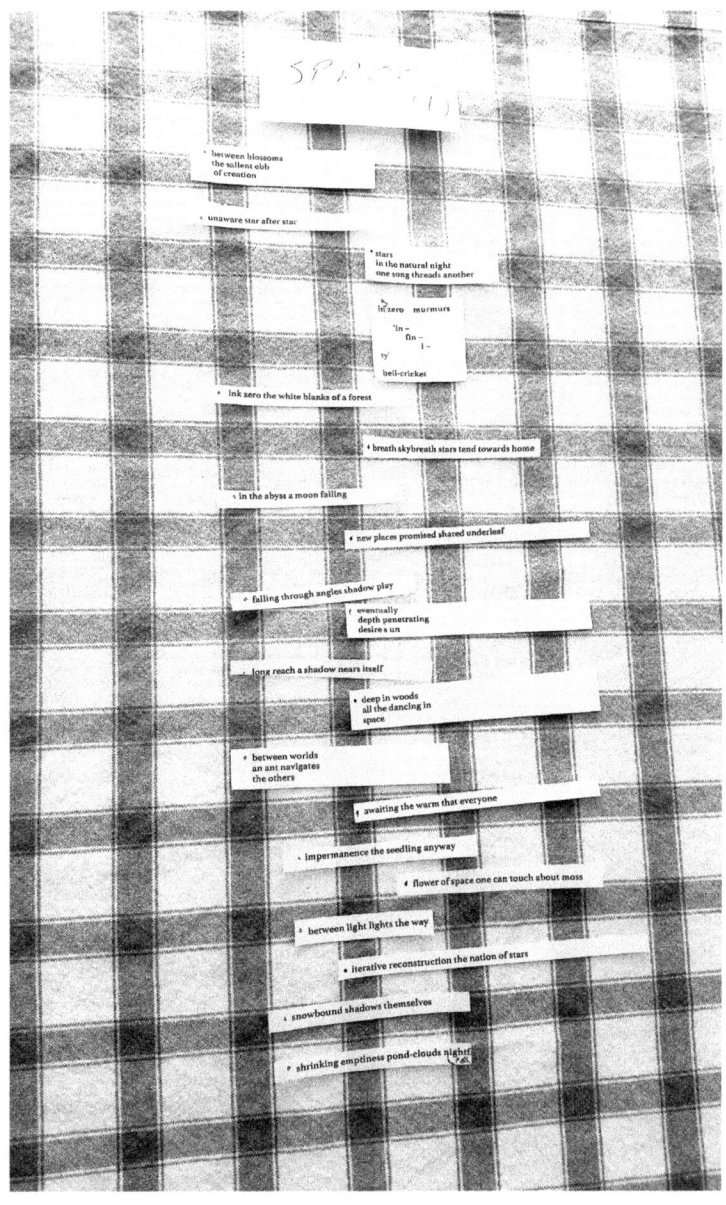

# Butterflies and Bones
(Matter)

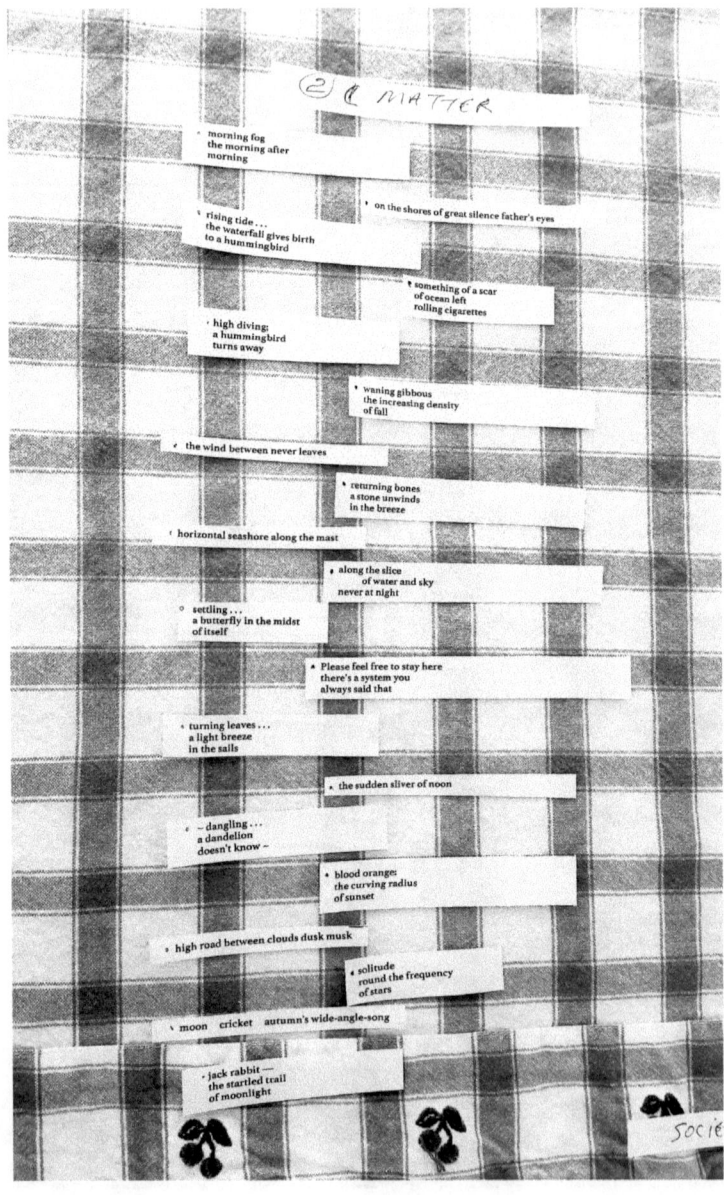

2 ( MATTER

morning fog
the morning after
morning

rising tide . . .
the waterfall gives birth
to a hummingbird

on the shores of great silence father's eyes

something of a scar
of ocean left
rolling cigarettes

high diving:
a hummingbird
turns away

waning gibbous
the increasing density
of fall

the wind between never leaves

returning bones
a stone unwinds
in the breeze

horizontal seashore along the mast

along the slice
of water and sky
never at night

settling . . .
a butterfly in the midst
of itself

Please feel free to stay here
there's a system you
always said that

turning leaves . . .
a light breeze
in the sails

the sudden sliver of noon

– dangling . . .
a dandelion
doesn't know –

blood orange:
the curving radius
of sunset

high road between clouds dusk musk

solitude
round the frequency
of stars

moon   cricket   autumn's wide-angle-song

jack rabbit —
the startled trail
of moonlight

# Bamboo Slam
(Slam)

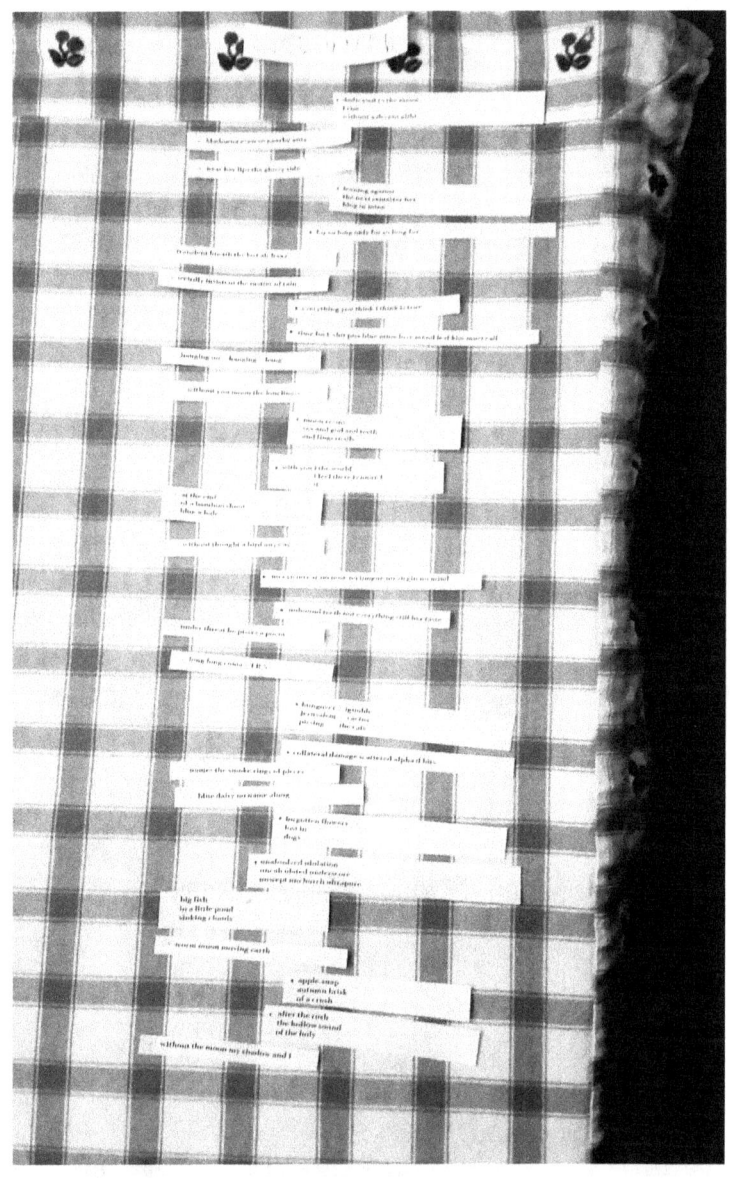

# The Table
(Creation)

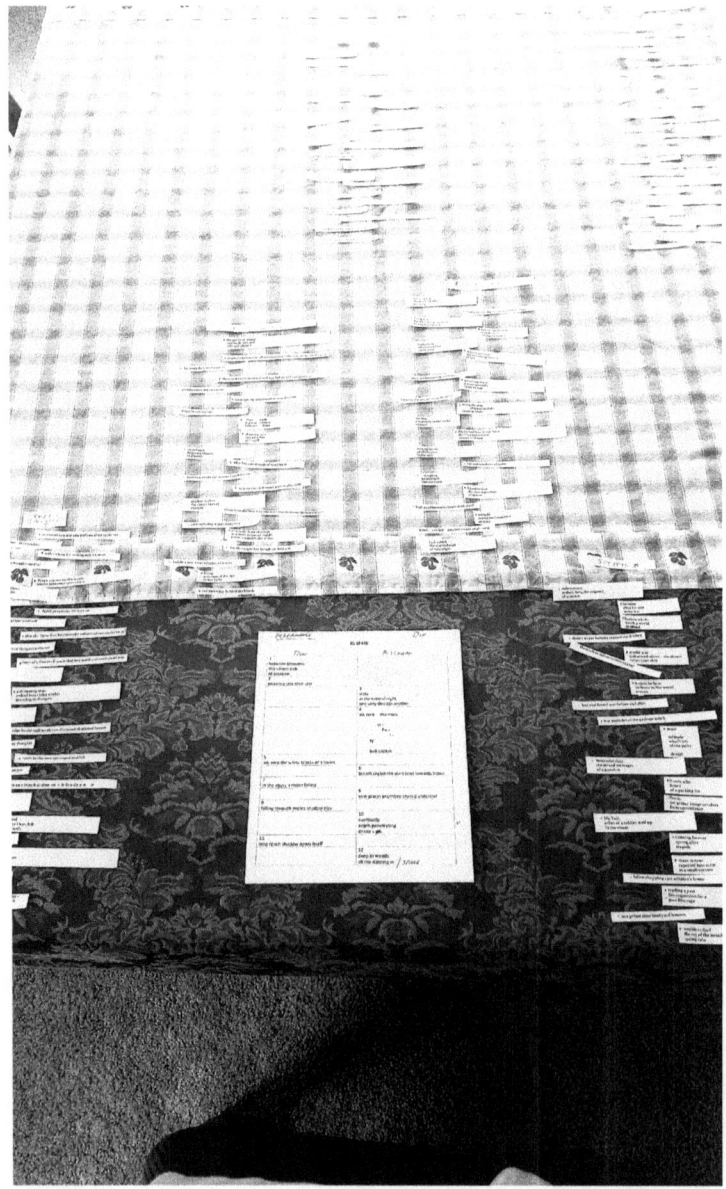

# Decanter Haiku
(Another Time -- Another Place -- Another Project)

www.ingramcontent.com/pod-product-compliance
Lightning Source LLC
Chambersburg PA
CBHW071721090426
42738CB00009B/1834